LOVE, AGONY AND A SCINTILLA OF HOPE

BK

notionpress.com

INDIA · SINGAPORE · MALAYSIA

Copyright © Bharath Krishnan M N 2024
All Rights Reserved.

ISBN   979-8-89133-858-6

"Life is a wild gamble."

Contents

Prologue

It was a cloudy day, and everyone inside the gallery enjoyed the warmth radiating from the exquisite paintings displayed on its walls. The curator of the gallery spoke to the crowd with a gentle voice and a smiling face. He was a calm man—quite elegant in his forties. He said to the awestruck crowd that the paintings were created by an artist who lived unnoticed in their small town for a major portion of his life.

1

The Empty Canvas

An old artist used to live in this town.

I often saw this miserable man in rags going on errands

and wondered what made him so sad and dejected.

Are all artists miserable?

He walked down the streets with a wry smile,

invariably drunk and talking to himself.

He always carried a dusty canvas

devoid of a single stroke of art,

empty like a broken heart.

One day I saw him at the park with a flock of pigeons.

For those birds, it seemed happiness was

in the stale bread crumbs he gave them.

After spending a stagnant day in haste,

I returned to the lake to bid adieu to the sun;

and there he was again

with his canvas mounted on a stand,

gazing at the crimson sky.

"Why is your canvas always empty?"

I asked him.

"I'm trying to remember a long-forgotten face,"

he said, smiling.

That smile was familiar,

twilight reflected in his grey eyes.

Gradually, the stage witnessed the union
of two passionate loners.
Days went on like a wild horse,
changes were everywhere,
but his canvas was still empty.

One winter night,
we drank together at his place—
a shabby and stinking room it was.
We drank and sang our hearts out,
talked about everything,
from the stars to the man,
laughed till our stomachs ached.
He was so bright; even the heavenly
stars gleamed in jealousy.

The next day when I woke up
I saw a vague portrait staring at me;
it was incomplete,
but those eyes were so full of life.

Near the canvas on the rusty chair

sat the old artist frozen,

peacefully dead with a smiling face.

It was a revealing moment;

life and death in such close proximity.

A serene winter morning awaited me outside.

I looked at the paintings

that hung on the dirty walls.

There were portraits, but none

had those mystic eyes.

Who was he trying to remember?

Why did the end strike so sudden?

Questions remained.

No! I didn't need answers;

answers often led to disappointments.

I looked at him one last time;

his cold face seemed happy.

In all his works there was a

visible incompleteness.

This unique incompleteness

set him apart,

Just like me.

...

2

The Endless Road

On that dying tree sits a young bird
quiet and still, gazing to the heavens.

Black clouds conquer the sky.
The day turns as dark as my eyes
but now I should keep going,
for I have made the choice.

Ah! There comes my friend with his guitar
to make my day splendid with his rhythm.

I can see him at the window expecting me.
I should get there before the rain.

Why is he taking so long? Hurry, my friend!

The guitar case on my back constantly weighs me down;
a load of hope and guilt.

Which song should we play together
to celebrate my victory? I'm confused.

I still remember the days—

the evening of our marriage,

the morning she gave birth to my son;

that adorable little thing often goes to sleep craving a piece of bread.

And Stella; she's a goddess! I've let her down as well.

She suffers.

Smiles with heavy eyes and cries all alone in the dark.

Should I tell him that I'm about to leave this town

for some unknown land where I can live unnoticed?

Let him take my guitar and my savings too,

for I wish to roam as a worthless man in search of the last sunrise.

Should I continue on this dreadful path?

Indeed dreadful; but I see a glimmer of hope

that crosses all boundaries of morality and guilt.

This is inevitable.

Now he'll be amazed to discover himself

taking my position at the carnival.

We started off at the same time but it seems

I've fallen behind and he'll make it to the finish.

I've made all the arrangements.

Fly high, partner!

But what good is wealth and fame

without a single soul to share his warmth and happiness?

I've felt his loneliness—it will eventually rob him of his life.

Even his music shall be forgotten.

Rain will reign very soon and

as usual, I can see the small shabby bird

on that branch staring at the sky without the slightest shudder.

I believe, with the rain, something else seeped into its mind.

Something so valuable that it quenched its terrible thirst.

Oh, little bird,

if I had known your language we could've talked.

I think we'll have somewhat similar stories to boast about.

Loneliness is a virtuous bridge that connects only the blessed.

I should represent our troupe at the Great Music Carnival,

which shall lift me out of this treacherous pit.

But it seems I'm less worthy than my companion.

By now, he'll be at the entrance;

Let me fix his drink—he is probably tired.

I've reached this far and rain is about to pour.

Ah! He's at the door;

"Just hold on, partner!"

- THE DOOR OPENS -

"Come in! Let's celebrate."

"Your victory!"

"Ah! Ah! My victory, yours too."

Indeed. I have to win for I'm tired of losing.
Let me put my guitar case on your table.

"Cheers!"

- BOTH DRINKS-

"You seem to be troubled; what is it, partner,
that robbed you of your smile?
What has made you so silent?"

- DRINKS AGAIN -

I should speak.
"Something very odd to perceive
is flourishing inside of me;
l can feel it right at the centre of my heart."

- WALKS TOWARDS THE TABLE -

"I still cannot figure out,
is it oblivion or clarity guiding me through this wild wave of events,
events that I often fail to command?"

- UNLATCHES THE GUITAR CASE -

I should get this over with before it's too late.
I'll ask him for a cigarette.
"Hey! Can I get a cigarette?"

"I'll give you two."

He turns around to get the pack.
Now is the time
to take the sledgehammer out of the case,
Drive it swiftly to the side of his skull, crack it open,
And let him splash through the crevice.
Thus salvation.

It was just a matter of seconds;
he fell to the floor in a flash.
One of his teeth hit my toe and
woke me from my bloody trance.

He lay dead in a pool of blood;
traces of his lifeless brain on the floor mat.

The first drop touched the ground.
Soon rain took charge and I could smell the wet soil—
the mysterious scent of heavenly origin.

I peeped out of his window and saw this small bird
perched on a dead branch,
drenched in rain,
looking straight into my eyes.
What is it that you see?
Is it guilt or hope?

Amid the mess, I searched his place,
Fished out some cash and some wine.

Had his loneliness ceased to exist,
I wondered, or is this just the beginning of eternal misery?

- TEN MILES AWAY -

A loud roar woke Stella from her nap.

She looked out through the narrow window

and heaved a sigh of relief;

her beloved had been spared and her child was fast asleep.

He seemed happy.

Tears rolled down from her innocent eyes,

Gently caressing her cheeks, falling to her chest.

The hill came down and took them.

The rain never gave up.

- AND WE TRAVEL BACK -

He wrapped the cash in plastic

and stepped out into the rain.

For an instant, he felt a pain in his chest.

He longed to hug his wife and kiss her

and thus to unburden his heart.

But he never knew those gentle lips were by then

Lifeless and shattered.

He walked down the streets reflecting on his actions,
felt the cash in his breast pocket and dreamt of a new life.
Dreamt of a life that no longer existed.
Longed for the warmth of his home, which no longer existed.

Hope sometimes can be deceptive
and this man was its latest prey.
I flew over him, but he never noticed
the sole witness of his actions;
I felt pity for him, for he was as helpless as
a bird that was generously freed from its cage,
that does not know where to fly and where to perch.
For that bird, flying until its wings break is the only option.

From all that I've seen, I could tell that
sometimes men cannot die.
All they can do is keep walking.
And so he kept walking on the endless road,
embracing the raindrops
that fell on his chest.

3

Fare-Thee-Well

"Where have you gone?"
"Why is this world so dark when I'm awake?"
She never heard me scream,
and I could never emerge from the foggy tunnel—
tears blurred my vision and my feet trembled.
"God! Bless me with light, for I'm scared of
this never-ending oblivion."

She sat on a floating rock
in the midst of infinite lavender blooms,
facing the looming void.
I kept running towards her desperately.
With each step, her melody grew more distinct,
the same old bliss that once kissed my heart.
She was a distant hope;
yet this everlasting distance
kept her in close vicinity.

Now I could see her; with the mouth organ—
close to her breath, gently touching her lips.
For a blink, she saw me too.

I saw this dream over and over,
I could hear her song echoing around.
The sweet lavender scent, her dull yellow gown
and wavering hair made me restless.
Thanks to the dream, I never
forgot the light—
the remnant of a long-lost life.
I no longer remember the details, but
that one day still shines bright in my heart.
The day I met the deepest shade of your eyes,
the day reality paused for us to blink.

The day I came running to the stage
through the packed music hall
only to take in the last notes of your song.
I could see your bright smile,
even from the very last row.
"How was it?"
"Just like your eyes, love!"
Indeed, your eyes were as pristine as the twilight sky.

I never got to say goodbye then; and now,
I miss your song and your softest gaze.

Am I real or just a playful thought of yours?

She sat on the rock playing her mouth organ,
gazing into the alluring confusion—
waiting for her love to emerge through the void.

Now she can finally see her beloved,
struggling through the vicious fog;
but it was time, and let her wake up
from this fateful dream.

The sheets were soaked with sweat.
She lay with open eyes, terrified and disappointed,
in her damp room with dusty windows.

Beyond the grey walls, the night was calm and lonely,
with homeless souls on the moonlit streets.
Tears filled her eyes as memories sang their
long-forgotten songs loud and clear,
forcing a faint smile on her black lips
and a novel weight on her eyelids.

Moonlight seeped through the walls and
filled her room with its glory;
her eyes opened wide in anguish to see
herself surrounded by young lavender blooms—
brimming with life and joy,
below an elegant golden sky.

Now, I can see the light and my path—
and it seems a lifetime of darkness
is coming to an end and a humble beginning
is waiting to be embraced.

The heavenly stars looked down at her
With damp eyes and trembling lips.
She stared into the endless;
paused, smiled and moved her lips—
"I can see you finally!"

Epilogue

1

The protagonist walked towards a heap of ruins where once his home had been.

He was numb with pain and could no longer remain there. So he left behind his hometown, his heart heavy with guilt and grief. All along the way, he could hear his friend's music and could see his wife and child playing by the lakeside; all that he had lost reminded him of the weight of existence he was destined to live with. After days of travel, he came to a new town. A town with a calm population and serene weather.

2

The money he had in his breast pocket (wrapped in plastic) kept him going and helped him get a job at a local library. He spent the evenings at the lakeside park, and it was here that he met an old artist and his friendly pigeons. He was a shabby man in his late fifties, with a long white beard and a pair of weak eyes doped with despair.

As days went by, they met more often, and gradually a glimmer of light lit up their dark lives. A friendship even they could not fully comprehend.

One winter night, they drank together at the artist's place.

The old artist woke up suddenly at a late hour and hurried to his canvas. After a very long time, it seemed to him that he was certain about the face he had to bring to life onto his canvas.

He somehow fathomed that those were his final hours, but nothing stopped his swiftly moving paintbrush. His heart became heavier with each passing minute as his favourite memory manifested before him slowly but in a startlingly definitive manner.

He could only complete painting her eyes.

The next day, our protagonist found the old artist dead near an incomplete portrait.

He didn't know what to do. After pausing for a moment, he took down all the paintings that hung on the artist's walls, also the incomplete portrait, packed them and went out. As he was about to leave, he turned and looked at the artist one last time—"Farewell, dear friend."

3

"He never said goodbye."

Some said he left in a boat, some argued he fell from the cliff. Everyone had their versions. But no one actually knew where he went.

Henry was ten when he first met Julia. They went to the same city school.

"We should look for an abode on a hill, with clouds and mist passing us all the time," Julia said in her gentlest tone.

"I'll make a garden of roses and lavenders and vivid butterflies. There, among the flowers, I'll play a melody with my harmonica just for you to listen to."

"Will you paint me in my favourite yellow gown?"

Henry smiled.

Love is most beautiful when it blossoms at a young age, and just like that they sang and danced to their love songs and cherished every fleeting moment with tender hugs and gentle words.

While it had something unusual waiting for them in its arsenal, destiny held them intimately together for about seven magnificent years, years of joy, laughter and unwavering passion.

They had a beautiful story—a story in which a major part was lost in longing.

Henry went missing from their town, and nobody had the faintest idea where he had gone.

Julia met him for the last time on the festival day. She regretted not being able to bid him a proper farewell when they parted.

Later, her life was stagnant for years, yet time went on—season after season. She held on to the raging time, hopefully waiting for her beloved's return. No one saw or heard from Henry ever again.

Julia got a new lease on life when she crossed paths with a guitar luthier who offered her a second chance. He brought light and warmth back to her life. Julia later married him, and they had a beautiful daughter. She moved on with her life, but on some days, the memory of a garden of lavenders surrounded by mist and clouds made her eyes brim, and at those moments she thought about Henry and prayed he too had a perfect life somewhere.

4

Henry met James at a very strange time in his life. Dark days and depressing nights went around him in vicious circles, spiralling him slowly to an emotional arrest.

James was the new librarian in his town.

Soon they became close acquaintances. Henry's health and memories had been declining and it was clear that everything he was part of would cease in the coming days.

All his weariness and despair came to a sudden halt when James showed him a picture from his torn wallet of himself with his late wife and child. Stella reminded Henry of someone he had lost a long time ago. She had had the same stunning pair of eyes that Julia did.

"Your eyes are as pristine as the twilight sky," Henry had said when he met Julia on the festival day.

Through James, he came to know Stella's mother, who had been ill for a long time.

After the death of her husband, Julia lapsed into a chronic lung illness that made it extremely hard for her to breathe.

5

Humanity has a peculiar relationship with certain memories, some close-to-heart, warm memories that can both knock you off your feet and bring you back from the gallows. Distinct memories of Julia had exited his mind a long time ago, leaving behind traces of a long-lost life, like broken glass pieces hinting at a beautiful structure that had existed in the past.

The day James came for a drink to Henry's, they chatted about a vast range of subjects. Slowly, like a comforting breeze, James spoke about Stella's mother, her hometown, and her beauty when she had been a young woman.

"He was so bright that even the heavenly stars gleamed with jealousy," James thought to himself.

Henry slept late that day, only to wake up startled by a strange dream—he saw Julia in her garden of lavenders. She was playing her harmonica and eagerly waiting for him. But suddenly her music ceased and everything went black. He felt an increase in the pace of his breath and noticed that he was uncontrollably perspiring. He could sense it—he was about to face the ultimate truth.

He vigorously rummaged through his desk, looking for his paintbrush, and, finding it, set the canvas on its stand. In no time, he could see a pair of lively eyes manifesting on his canvas, which had remained empty for so long.

She looked at him with wide eyes and sparkling cheeks. When Henry hugged her for the first time, she leaned towards him to reach his lips. Their breaths embraced, their trembling lips yearned for a union, but they never kissed.

The sky, the wind and the entirety of reality caressed them and sang a marvellous song of eternal love.

Henry finally remembered this gorgeous stare of hers during his last moments, and so he drew that wide, beautiful pair of eyes that reflected an entire universe of passion, just as his breath left its abode.

6

She saw him struggling towards her. There was some inexplicable void dragging him backwards, but nothing was strong enough to stop him. Slowly, the sky above her garden turned golden and all the lavender blooms started humming her favourite music. He came closer and it seemed to her that a lifetime of longing was coming to a satisfying end. Thus, she took her last breath peacefully immersed in her surreal dream without knowing that, somewhere far away yet spellbindingly close, Henry too had a peaceful and satisfying moment of realization.

7

People are mysteriously alluring puzzles floating around in this eternal ocean of reality. Each one busy travelling down a crowded street, impatiently struggling to get to a definite destination. Yes, all of us have to reach the same place ultimately, but none of us can take the same path. For some, the path may be distinct, while for others it may be oblivious, but gradually life unites us in a very poetic fashion. James, the guitarist, Henry, Stella, Julia, everyone had their missing pieces, pieces that made them beautiful puzzles.

Incompleteness can sometimes be perceived as beautiful, because when something reaches a full circle—when it completes itself—it can be judged, but never can an incomplete poem be judged as good or bad, it just remains, with no end.

If James had not chosen that dreadful path, he could have been killed in the landslide that took his wife and child, leaving no one to greet the pain in Henry's eyes and relieve him of a lifetime of despair. If not for James, Henry would never have attempted Julia's portrait or dreamt of their golden garden or accompanied her in her final dream.

In a way, Henry passed on his art to James, who took it to the world and built himself a new life. People deserve to live better; despair and poverty should never hold them back.

The guitarist came full circle. He enjoyed fame and earned wealth and was so tired of his lonely life that he decided to pass on his legacy to his friend. James, on the other hand, enjoyed nothing. His life was barren—*"devoid of a single stroke of art"*—and hope tainted his free will. He was forced to choose the wrong way to get to the right end. Stella and his son definitely deserved better, but the cosmos has a unique way of maintaining order. It had to show James the irony of life, and it showed him this in the hardest way a husband and a father could imagine.

Sorrow consumed James all along, but somewhere deep down, in some dark corner of his heart, there was a sense of freedom that liberated him from the clutches of depression; he had his life, and that was a true blessing. James thus decided to live and, in this way, preserve the warm memories of Stella and his son all through his journey, until he greeted them with eyes full of tears and a heart abounding with love. Henry, through his art, thus gave James a second chance to live and in turn a sense of purpose with which to float around on this eternal ocean.

8

Life is a wild gamble. The closer you look, the wilder it gets.

"The day reality paused for us to blink."

Julia hopefully scanned the crowd, to meet his eyes.

Henry rushed towards the stage but was abruptly halted by the sound of a woman's muffled cry and a child's soft snore. Gradually, the cheerful sounds around him subsided, giving way to a deafening crushing noise. He felt as if the entire world was trembling around him, but he was surprised since everyone else seemed calm. The next instant, he heard a sound similar to that of a wing flap and it seemed to emerge from the stage where Julia was playing the concluding notes of her harmonica.

His perceptions turned violent like a turbulent sea, and soon it became unbearable for him to hold on. He smiled with teary eyes when Julia asked him about her music—he never heard her song.

Suddenly, all the noises ceased and everything was calm. He was temporarily blinded by the bright lights he was later exposed to, and it was very late when he realized his ears were bleeding and skin burning. His eyelids could no longer withstand the violent flashes of unseen colours. After about an instant, he opened his eyes to a beautiful lake with crimson waters. He immediately noticed a sparrow on his skinny right shoulder.

Who could explain to him how, in a sudden moment, he had flipped to an alternate existence, in which his skin was wrinkled and back slightly bent, how he came to a lakeside park with a hungry flock of pigeons compassionately fluttering around him, hoping for the bread in his weak right hand?

Could anyone console him for the beautiful life he had lost?

Thus, Henry came to the unknown town, where he was not noticed or cared about for years. Along the way, he created numerous paintings, most of them with a brilliant mix of colours.

9

After Henry's death, James established a small art gallery, where he showcased Henry's brilliantly vivid paintings. It was the beginning of an era in which people started to study rather than enjoy art, and thus James' art gallery, with its unique and abstract paintings, gained widespread attention.

Artists from around the globe came down to this small town to study the arresting choice of colours in the paintings. Critics soon began decrypting messages the anonymous creator had hidden within the layers of his paintings. Ironically, they never ever realized that all those messages and codes had been simple and unintended brush strokes.

Every single man and woman searched for meaning that was never present. No one actually tried to understand the works of a broken man, who was confused to the very last moment of his own life, an artist who roamed aimlessly around the town in search of a reason to remain alive.

The art gallery that showcased the works of an anonymous artist eventually became famous and made a good fortune for its curator—James.

Among Henry's works, three paintings were left unattended by the world, for they were considered too direct to require decoding: the painting in which a young girl clutched a harmonica in her right hand, impatiently looking away from the observer, the one featuring a man walking in the rain with his right palm in his coat pocket and a small bird hovering above him, and the third was an incomplete portrait—just a pair of eyes.

James remained puzzled when he wondered how in the world Henry had drawn a picture of him walking in the rain on that fateful day. How was that even possible? Henry was only a later episode in James's life—that rainy day had been far before their union.

"No, I should never wish for an answer. Let it be as it is, for knowing too much can break down even the strongest of men," James consoled himself.

A Random Page in James' Diary

Today, when I look back to the roads I have travelled, I feel a sense of pride for not quitting. I had all the reasons to do so, but I chose to live on. Do I have to fear that one day people around me shall chase me out, as they do with murderers? Will I have to encounter such a day?

Nowadays I seldom think of Stella and our son. Does that make me a sinner? Is that vile, leaving behind the memory of my dead wife and son and hoping for a new start? My childhood and adulthood were spent in dismay and poverty, I was just a mediocre musician by profession, the world is not for the mediocre—it just needs the excellent ones and I'm becoming one of them now.

Years ago, on a cold night, I had a nightmare and when I woke up all I could see was darkness, but piercing that darkness came a muffled cry. I listened without moving an inch. It was her... Stella had the sweetest voice in the whole world. I did not try to console her, I just listened... A strange chill wrapped itself around us that night. It was in that instant, that devilish idea flashed through my mind. I found hope in that idea. That idea caressed me back to my peaceful sleep.

I can never ever make up for what I did to my friend, I never wish to. Come what may in hell, but this day... this moment, I'm alive... and as long as I'm alive, I deserve a good life, I deserve to be loved.

Somewhere, away from all the known planes and barriers of reality, the comforting rays of a golden sun caressed the slanting roof of an abode surrounded by silver clouds creating a surreal canopy over a garden with fluttering butterflies. From that garden, a gentle symphony of a harmonica arose, gradually, along with the scent of lavenders and roses.